UNDERSTANDING MYTHS

CHINESE MYTHS

MEGAN KOPP

Crabtree Publishing Company

www.crabtreebooks.com

Author: Megan Kopp
Publishing plan research and development:
    Sean Charlebois, Reagan Miller
    Crabtree Publishing Company
Editor-in-chief: Lionel Bender
Editors: Simon Adams, Lynn Peppas
Proofreaders: Laura Booth, Wendy Scavuzzo
Project coordinator: Kathy Middleton
Photo research: Kim Richardson
Designer: Ben White
Cover design: Margaret Amy Salter
Production coordinator and Prepress technician:
    Margaret Amy Salter
Production: Kim Richardson
Print coordinator: Katherine Berti

Consultants: Noreen Doyle, M.A. Egyptology, M.A. Nautical Archaeology, B.A. Anthropology, Art, and Classical Civilizations: Author and consultant, Maine; and Amy Leggett-Caldera, M.Ed., Elementary and Middle School Education Consultant, Mississippi State University.

Cover: A pagoda in the Summer Palace (top center); a carving of Chinese mythical warriors (top background); a statue showing the Jade Emperor (bottom center); golden Chinese dragons (bottom left and right)
Title page: A statue of a protector lion in the Forbidden City of Beijing

Photographs and reproductions:
Maps: Stefan Chabluk
Front cover: Shutterstock
The Art Archive: 5t (Genius of China Exhibition), 5b (National Palace Museum Taiwan), 6b (National Palace Museum Taiwan), 9 (Bibliothèque Nationale Paris), 15 (Genius of China Exhibition), 21 (British Library), 24 (Musée Cernuschi Paris/Gianni Dagli Orti), 25 (British Museum), 26, 27 (Musée Cernuschi Paris/Gianni Dagli Orti), 28, 30 (Musée Guimet Paris / Gianni Dagli Orti), 31 (Bibliothèque Municipale Versailles/Kharbine-Tapabor/Coll. Jean Vigne), 37 (Musée Guimet Paris/Gianni Dagli Orti) •
The Kobal Collection: 44 (China Film Group Corporation) •
shutterstock.com: 1 (Hung Chung Chih), 4, 6t (WICHAN KONGCHAN), 10t (Philip Lange), 10b (zhaoliang70), 13r (tratong), 16b (Jan Kowalski), 19 (sathienput), 22 (Venus Angel), 22 (Hung Chung Chih), 33r (yienkeat), 34t (Gwoeii), 36 (skphotography), 38–39 (meanmachine77), 40t (JEEPNEX), 40b (mary416), 41 (mamahoohooba), 42–43 (123Nelson), 43t (Paul McKinnon), 42b (stewie), 44 (any_keen) •
Topfoto (The Granger Collection): 13, 17, 23, 33b, 34r, 35, 39; (topfoto.co.uk): 8 (World History Archive), 11 (Charles Walker), 12 (The British Library/HIP), 18 (Mel Longhurst), 32 (Fine Art Images/Heritage-Images) • Werner Forman Archive: 14 (Private Collection), 16t (Christian Deydier, London).

This book was produced for Crabtree Publishing Company by Bender Richardson White

---

Library and Archives Canada Cataloguing in Publication

Kopp, Megan
    Understanding Chinese myths / Megan Kopp.

(Myths understood)
Includes index.
Issued also in electronic formats.
ISBN 978-0-7787-4507-5 (bound).--ISBN 978-0-7787-4512-9 (pbk.)

    1. Mythology, Chinese--Juvenile literature. 2. China--Religion--Juvenile literature. I. Title. II. Series: Myths understood

BL1825.K66 2012   j398.20951   C2011-908369-8

Library of Congress Cataloging-in-Publication Data

Kopp, Megan.
 Understanding Chinese myths / Megan Kopp.
   p. cm. -- (Myths understood)
 Includes index.
 ISBN 978-0-7787-4507-5 (reinforced library binding : alk. paper) -- ISBN 978-0-7787-4512-9 (pbk. : alk. paper) -- ISBN 978-1-4271-7900-5 (electronic pdf) -- ISBN 978-1-4271-8015-5 (electronic html)
 1. Mythology, Chinese--Juvenile literature. 2. China--Religion--Juvenile literature. I. Title.

BL1825.K667 2012
299.5'1113--dc23

                                        2011050091

Crabtree Publishing Company
www.crabtreebooks.com   1-800-387-7650

Printed in Canada/062012/TR20120518

Published in Canada
Crabtree Publishing
616 Welland Ave.
St. Catharines, Ontario
L2M 5V6

Published in the United States
Crabtree Publishing
PMB 59051
350 Fifth Avenue, 59th Floor
New York, New York 10118

Published in the United Kingdom
Crabtree Publishing
Maritime House
Basin Road North, Hove
BN41 1WR

Published in Australia
Crabtree Publishing
3 Charles Street
Coburg North
VIC 3058

CONTENTS

WHAT ARE MYTHS?

Myths are ancient stories that have been passed down through many generations of people. Many of these stories are so old, that they began as spoken tales. Myths are stories that have helped people make sense of their lives for thousands of years.

Without myths, ancient people would have been unable to explain unknowns. Topics such as the creation of Earth, the Sun, and the stars, the origins of humankind, and life and death, would have been almost impossible for them to understand. Myths also shaped their beliefs and **traditions**.

CHINESE MYTHOLOGY

In the early days of China's history, myths helped explain such things as where people came from and how they could succeed and flourish. They taught people how they should act in society, and how they could work to overcome such challenges as floods. Myths brought order to chaos.

Because myths were originally spoken stories, they changed as they were passed on. In Chinese **mythology**, there are different ideas about the creation of the

CHINESE STORYTELLING

In the Chinese language, a myth is called a *shen-hua.* This means "sacred story." At first, these stories were spoken and passed down by word of mouth. The first written record of them was in *Questions of Heaven*, written between 400 and 300 B.C.E.

universe and there are at least four different flood myths. The name of the main character in different myths often changes. There are usually several names—You Xiong, Huangdi, Yellow Emperor—and many different versions of the same name—Pan Gu, Pangu, Pank'u—for the central figure. It was only when most Chinese myths were written down in ancient texts, during the Age of the Philosophers from 600 to 100 B.C.E, that they became more consistent.

The Classic of Mountains and Seas is a collection of myths written down between the 200s B.C.E. and the 100s C.E. It is the most complete collection of Chinese myths in existence, including stories of more than 200 **mythical** figures.

Left: A pottery tomb guardian wearing armor and a phoenix headdress trampling on a demon, made in the early 700s C.E.

Below: This 11th-century C.E. silk handscroll shows Emperor Min Huang's epic journey to an area of China called Shu (modern Sichuan).

MYTHS TODAY

Epic heroes and fantastic tales continue to be shared in literature, movies, and even comic books. In her books *The Joy Luck Club* and *The Kitchen God's Wife*, Chinese-American author Amy Tan draws on Chinese mythical and family traditions and their impact on a generation of Chinese-Americans. The popular Disney children's movie, *Mulan* is based on a Chinese mythical character of a female warrior. One of Jackie Chan's best movies is *The Myth*, a fantasy adventure drawing on ancient myths. Chinese-American filmmaker Ang Lee entertained the world with his legendary folktale *Crouching Tiger, Hidden Dragon*. *Chinese Mythology* is a current comic series in China that shows mythical stories of ancient **kingdoms** as cartoons.

ANCIENT CHINA

China has almost 4,000 years of written history but its ancient civilization goes back well before that. In China in 1929, archaeologists uncovered part of a human skull. Peking Man, as he was called, lived in that part of the world from 700,000 to 200,000 years ago.

Remains of one of the first settled **cultures** were found along the river valleys of northern China. The culture is known as the Yangshao and dates from 5000 to 3000 B.C.E. In **Prehistoric China**, people farmed the soil, created pottery, and lived in small villages. The Longshan people, who lived from around 3000 to 2200 B.C.E., were the first to build cities. This is the time of such mythical rulers as Fu Xi and Shen Nong.

WHAT IS A DYNASTY?

In China's past, leadership was decided by force. Family groups—or clans—fought each other for control of a region. Powerful clans formed dynasties, in which a series of leaders came from the same clan.

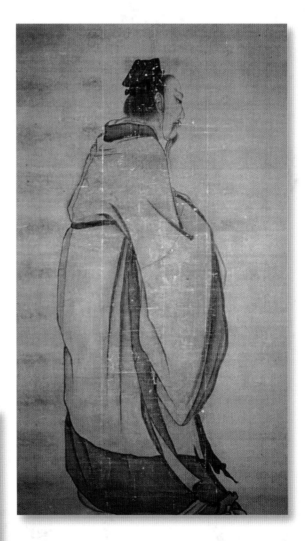

Above: Emperor Wu was a wise ruler during the Zhou Dynasty of 1121–221 B.C.E.

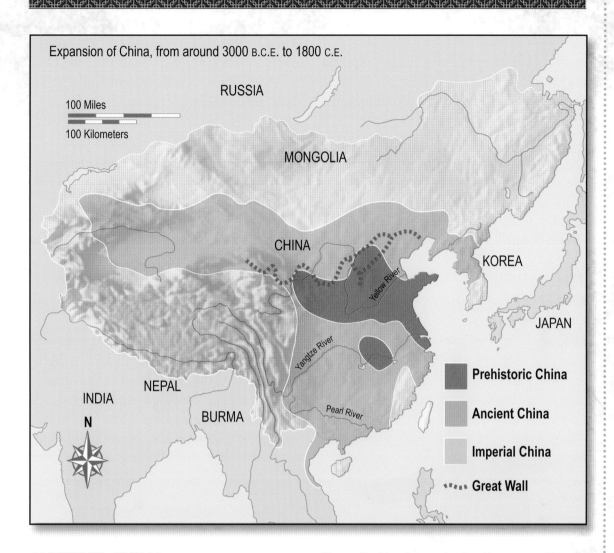

Expansion of China, from around 3000 B.C.E. to 1800 C.E.

100 Miles

100 Kilometers

RUSSIA

MONGOLIA

CHINA

Yellow River

KOREA

JAPAN

Yangtze River

NEPAL

INDIA

N

BURMA

Pearl River

Prehistoric China

Ancient China

Imperial China

Great Wall

ANCIENT CHINA

Ancient China refers to the period from 2205 B.C.E. to 221 B.C.E. During this time, mythological stories began to merge with history. The Xia Dynasty ruled China, but no written records exist from this period.

The Shang Dynasty took over in 1766 B.C.E. During their rule, a form of writing was developed on oracle bones (see page 8). In Ancient China, people believed in **gods**. Kings always looked to the gods for advice before taking action. They consulted oracle

Above: Prehistoric peoples lived in eastern China. Ancient Chinese kings extended their rule south and west before the birth of **Imperial China** in 221 B.C.E.

bones to provide answers to questions. In 1121 B.C.E., the Shang were overthrown by the Zhou, who said that the Shang king was corrupt. Using oracle bones for guidance, the Zhou claimed that the Sky God, Di, had passed his authority to the Zhou. The Zhou ruled for 900 years. Many myths were written down in that time.

IMPERIAL CHINA

Imperial China is probably the best-known period in China's history. It begins with the Qin Dynasty in 221 B.C.E. and ends when the Qing Dynasty was overthrown in 1911 C.E. The difference between the Qin Dynasty, and the Xia, Shang, and Zhou dynasties before it, is that the Qin Dynasty united all the states of China within one **empire**. During Imperial China, the state of Qin controlled all China.

THE EMPEROR

King Zheng was the ruler of the state of Qin. When he succeeded in taking control of all the other Chinese states, he changed his name to Shi Huangdi, which literally means "first emperor." The new emperor established the Qin—pronounced "Chin"—Dynasty in 221 B.C.E. The entire country was now given the name China.

Most Chinese **civil servants** inherited their jobs or were born into a trade before Shi Huangdi became emperor. He changed this system by choosing new officials based on their skills. This gave him greater control over the country. He set up one currency and system of measurements throughout the country to make **trade** easier. He ordered the creation of a writing system to be used only by the most highly educated people. He also ordered that all books be burned, except the ones he liked on medicine, agriculture, and foretelling of the future.

On Shi Huangdi's death in 210 B.C.E, a new emperor was chosen from his family. But the Qin Dynasty was short-lived. In 206 B.C.E., the Han Dynasty took power and ruled China until 220 C.E.

ORACLE BONES

In Ancient China, it was believed that turtle shells and some animal bones had a special connection with the gods. A difficult question that no one could answer was asked of the gods. The shell or bone was drilled, then heated until it cracked. A priest read the patterns of the cracks and found in them the answer to the question. A scholar then wrote down the god's answer on the bone.

Left: Shi Huangdi became the first emperor of the Qin Dynasty when he united the country under his leadership in 221 B.C.E.

坑儒焚書

EMPEROR YAO

Emperor Yao lived around 2300 B.C.E. He was the great-great-grandson of Huangdi, the Yellow Emperor. Yao is one of the five mythical emperors of prehistoric times. He was regarded by the scholar Confucius (550–478 B.C.E.) as a fine example of a good, honest, and unselfish person. According to myth, Yao was a kind and caring ruler. It was during his reign that order was made out of chaos (see page 12). Also, a great flood was controlled and one sun established in the sky. Yao is also remembered for not passing on his throne to his son. Yao did not believe his son was worthy of the title and gave the role to a peasant, Shun.

Above: Shi Huangdi lived from 259 to 210 B.C.E. In 221 B.C.E., he became the first Qin emperor. He ordered the burning of books and executed scholars who displeased him, as seen in this watercolor painted on silk.

RELIGION *AND* GODS

The Ancient Chinese believed that matter and energy were the same things. Mountains were made of energy in the form of rocks. Mountains have always played an important role in Chinese myths. It was believed that Five Sacred Peaks existed in the north, south, east, west, and center of China. Each peak was a direct link to heaven.

One of the earliest Chinese religions is Daoism, sometimes called Taoism. Tao is pronounced "dow" and means the "way" or "path." Daoism stressed the importance of people living simply and close to nature.

Both Daoism and Confucianism were introduced in the 400s B.C.E. Confucianism is based on the teachings of Confucius, a scholar who lived in China at that time. It was based on social order, loyalty to family and king, and **ancestor** worship. It became the state religion in 136 B.C.E.

Buddhism spread from India through east Asia and finally to China during the Han Dynasty. Buddhism teaches spiritual purity. Known as the Three Ways, the religions of Daoism, Confucianism, and Buddhism existed together in Han China.

XI WANG MU

Xi Wang Mu, or Queen Mother of the West, is an ancient Chinese **goddess** commonly associated with Daoism. She is mentioned on oracles bones dating back to the Shang Dynasty. She is known as the goddess of eternal life and is often shown wearing a hat fitted with the peaches of **immortality**.

Above: The Yungang grottoes in Shanxi, China, are ancient Buddhist **temple** caves. They are one of the most famous examples of Buddhist religious art.

THE EIGHT IMMORTALS

The Eight Immortals are the best-known characters in Chinese mythology. They are often shown as having a good time, but each has their own story of how they sought immortality.

The Heavenly Empress had a party after the harvest of the peaches of immortality—the ability to live forever. When it was time to go home, the Eight Immortals decided to cross the sea using their magical powers. Li Tieguai threw down his cane and surfed across the waves. Zhang Guo Lao rode his donkey. Zhongli Quan floated lazily on his fan. Han Xiangzi stepped into a basket and sailed away. Lu Dongbin used his magic sword. Cao Guojiu rode his jade tablet. He Xiangu drifted in her lotus flower. Lan Caihe played his flute, and he was lifted up from the ground by the air and taken away.

The son of the Dragon King, who lived under the sea, liked music. He sucked Lan down into the depths of the ocean. The other immortals went to Lan's rescue and pulled him from the sea, but his flute was lost. They lit a big fire to dry up the seas to find the instrument. As war raged, the gods took pity and returned the flute to Lan. They refilled the seas and restored peace.

Below: The Eight Immortals each have magical symbols—from fans to flutes—as shown in this illustration.

PAN GU CREATES THE WORLD

Long ago, the Chinese believed that Earth began in a state of chaos—a dark, shapeless mass of confusion. While there are many different creation myths, Pan Gu the Giant is the most popular.

At the beginning of time, Earth and the sky were lumped together in an egg-like mass. Pan Gu slept inside this dark lump for 18,000 years. When he awoke, he broke out of the egg. The lighter parts of the egg floated up and became heaven. The heavier parts joined together and became Earth. Pan Gu pushed heaven higher with his hands. His feet pushed Earth downward. Pan Gu grew into a giant as he pushed heaven and Earth apart. He stayed like this for 18,000 years and finally things stopped moving. Not long after, he felt very tired. He let go of heaven and lay down and died. His last breath became clouds. His eyes became the Sun and the Moon. His legs and arms became mountains. His blood turned to rivers. The hair on his body became trees and plants. His teeth and bones became rocks and minerals.

HORNED BEINGS

Chinese mythological figures, such as Pan Gu, are often shown with horns. Unlike western mythology, horned beings in Chinese mythology are linked with magical or supernatural powers that are used for good instead of evil. Horns are a sign of great power and strength.

Right: Pan Gu is a mythical Chinese figure linked with the creation of Earth. He is sometimes shown wearing leaves, as here.

Left: This oracle bone, made from a tortoise shell during the Shang Dynasty, is marked with Chinese characters that are answers to creation questions.

Wa, the creator of humankind. Nu Wa's companion is Fu Xi, the first mythical emperor of China. In their myths, the Chinese worshiped their emperors. They became wise and powerful gods. Fu Xi is said to have invented writing, tamed animals, and taught people to fish with nets and hunt with iron weapons.

Below: Yin and yang are drawn in harmony as the light and dark halves of a circle.

CREATION AND THE GODS

Ancient Chinese stories describe the origins of the world as a place with no light and no dark, no high and no low. It was empty, yet full of matter waiting to become a world. This idea is echoed in creation myths such as Pan Gu, who formed heaven and Earth. The concept of *yin* and *yang* is central to this myth. Yin and yang are a pair of perfect opposites such as light and dark, and man and woman. Together, they are one. They cannot exist without each other.

There are six different creation myths in Chinese mythology. One of the earliest myths is based on a female goddess, Nu

LINK TO TODAY

The Chinese believed that two opposite but matching forces make up all aspects of life. As one increases, the other decreases. The two are always in balance. The yin and yang symbol might be a fashion accessory today but it holds great meaning in Chinese society.

MORTALITY AND DEATH

Immortality was a common theme in Ancient Chinese myths. However, it was a difficult idea for most people to understand. They believed in **mortality** and saw that death was unavoidable. As a result, they believed that funerals were important events. For the wealthy, funerals became elaborate **rituals**. Efforts were made to preserve the dead body for as long as possible. Small pieces of jade—a semiprecious stone—were often placed under the tongue, then over the eyes and mouth to close them. It was believed that jade helped slow decay.

Ancient Shang tombs contain a treasure trove of information about Ancient Chinese beliefs and funeral traditions. Kings were buried with riches that included war chariots, often complete with horses and charioteers. Human **sacrifices** were made during this period. The remains of sacrificial victims have been found in Shang tombs. In special ceremonies, 10 victims at a time had their heads cut off.

During the early Zhou Dynasty, religion was largely based on the idea that each person had two souls: a physical soul and an eternal, or everlasting, soul. The eternal soul could be honored with rich offerings.

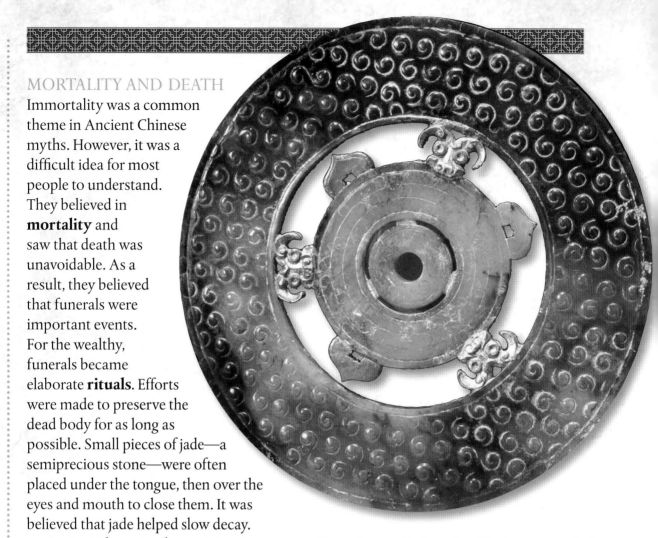

Above: Bronze objects such as this disc were symbolic of the sky and thought to represent the Sun.

MAWANGDUI BANNER

One of the most famous funeral **artifacts** from a tomb dated to the Han Dynasty is a T-shaped banner. Draped over the coffin, the elaborate banner shows the heavens and the underworld. The middle represents Earth. The god Nu Wa is shown in the heavens. There are also **cranes**—birds that are Daoist symbols of immortality.

THE TALE OF PENG ZU

In Chinese culture, taking charge of one's health through diet and exercise is a key to a long life. The myth of Peng Zu teaches this idea.

Peng Zu's mother's pregnancy lasted for three years. She grew bigger and bigger with each passing month. Finally she gave birth to six children. Peng Zu was one of the six. Peng Zu grew older and older and, when he was 700 years old, he did not look old at all. Some people said it was because of a natural medicine he took. Others said it was his special breathing exercises. But the truth was in the special chicken soup he made. Peng Zu's chicken soup was so good that he shared it with the Celestial Emperor. The emperor was delighted with the soup. It tasted good and made him happy. He rewarded Peng Zu with an 800-year life. When his time was up, Peng Zu was sad. He had lived a full life, but he was still not ready for it to end. Even 800 years was not enough.

Tombs from the Han Dynasty show a wide variety of goods that were placed in graves. The tomb of one wealthy woman contained small, wooden statues of her servants who would assist her in the afterlife. Her tomb also contained silk fabrics for clothing, and many dishes and containers.

Below: This jade funeral suit of princess Tou Wan, wife of Prince Liu Sheng, dates from the 100s B.C.E. It was found lying in her tomb in Mancheng, China.

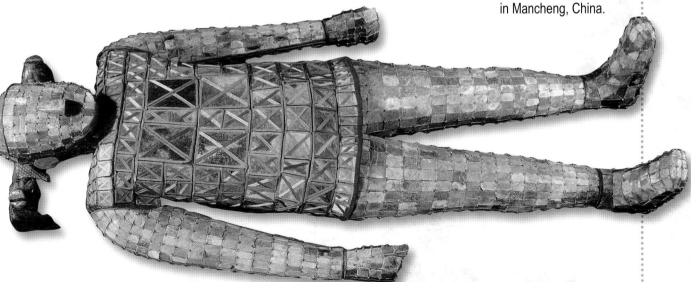

THE NATURAL WORLD

China is a vast country, with towering mountain peaks and wide fertile plains. Chinese civilization began next to its northern rivers, such as the Yellow River, and the land alongside rivers has always been farmed. As a result, many Chinese myths deal with the natural world and disasters such as floods.

In Ancient China, people assumed that the nature gods were in charge of the weather. Lei Shan was the god of thunder, Dian Mu the goddess of lightning, Yu Shi the god of rain. Farmers gave gifts to the gods in the hope that they would make the weather good for growing crops. They thought they could guess the will of the gods by observing natural events such as storms, the shape of clouds, and animal behavior.

Natural geography also played an important role in myths. The Chinese believed that mountains possessed great power and were home to many mythical animals and plants. Dragons spent the winter months resting in mountain caves.

LINK TO TODAY

The Harvest Moon or Mid-Autumn **Festival** is an ancient celebration held on the first full moon in mid-autumn. As in the past, farmers celebrate the harvest of vegetables, fruits, and grains they have grown during the year.

SACRED MOUNTAINS

In the Five Sacred Peaks myth, mountains mark the center of the world and the four points of the compass. Other mountains were also sacred. One of the peaks in the Kunlun Mountains was the home of the immortals.

Left: Chinese fields of rice, a grain grown in the country for thousands of years.

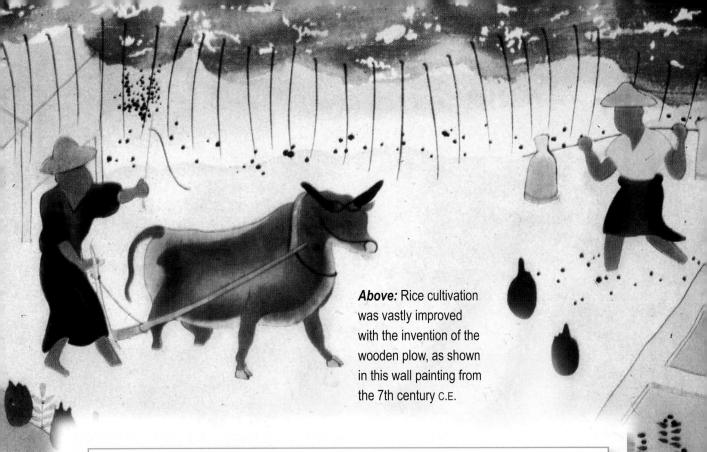

Above: Rice cultivation was vastly improved with the invention of the wooden plow, as shown in this wall painting from the 7th century C.E.

YAN DI—GOD OF AGRICULTURE

In prehistoric times, people hunted and gathered their food. When people settled along the fertile plains of northern China's river valleys and became farmers, their success allowed Chinese culture to flourish. The myth of the divine farmer was part of this.

Yan Di was the son of a princess. She gave birth to him after a close encounter with a dragon near the River Jiangshui. He had many names. For example, Jiang, after his birthplace, and Yiqi, his personal name. When he became the Fire Emperor, he was called Yan Di, but most people called him Shen Nong, the divine farmer. It is said that Shen Nong taught people how to use wooden plows to work the fields. He was always interested in plants. He learned that plants could be used as medicines, and started experimenting with them. Unfortunately, some of his experiments turned out to be poisonous and one day he died. Today, he is always portrayed with a black face—from the poison—and dressed in leaves.

ANIMALS AND PLANTS

Since ancient times, the Chinese have believed that both real and mythical creatures possessed certain values. The tortoise, for example, represented stability. In the myth of Nu Wa and Gong Gong, the heavens were supported by the legs of a tortoise. This allowed Nu Wa to repair the world that Gong Gong had destroyed.

Tigers were thought to be the kings of all the animals. Tiger ornaments, shaped from white jade, were worn by commanders of armies. They assisted and protected the commanders and their troops in battle. In many myths, emperors are linked with the image of a dragon. Dragons were often paired with the phoenix, or the empress. The beautiful phoenix only appeared in myths in times of good fortune. The Ancient Chinese divided the sky into four sections and named them after these four important creatures: the tortoise in the north, the tiger in the west, the dragon in the east, and the phoenix in the south.

Many mythical gods appear as half animal and half human. Both Nu Wa and Fu Xi have the bodies of snakes and the heads of humans.

Mythical plants also occur in ancient myths. The giant peach tree forms a ladder to the sky. The leaning mulberry holds 10 suns—one for each day in the 10-day week of Ancient China—in its branches after the Sun has passed through the sky.

Right: The mythical phoenix bird appeared at times of good fortune, but disappeared when times were hard or difficult.

DRAGONS

Dragons are symbols of great strength and power in Chinese culture. Chinese dragons do not breath fire. They are seen as protectors of the heavens and waterways. Dragons lived in the water and controlled the rain. During times of drought, the Chinese prayed to them. A traditional dragon or rain dance is still performed at Chinese New Year.

HOW THE JINGWEI BIRD FILLED THE SEA

The myth of the Jingwei bird teaches a common theme of metamorphosis, that is the changing from a human into another life form. It also shows that fathers must learn to control their children.

There once was a bird with a brightly colored head, white beak, red feet, and a "jingwei, jingwei" call. This was no ordinary bird. It was once the daughter of Emperor Yan Di. Cute and charming, the girl was spoiled by her father. She was allowed to go wherever she wanted. One day, she wandered away to the sea, where she found a boat and rowed out. A storm came up, swamped the boat, and she drowned. When night came, the emperor started a search, but did not find her. He saw the bird, but did not make the connection. For many years, the Jingwei bird flew from the western mountains to pick up twigs and pebbles, which it would drop in the eastern sea. Finally, the sea asked why the bird was doing it. The bird said she was angry that her life had been cut short, and she was going to fill the sea so that no one else would ever drown there. The sea laughed and told her she would never be able to fill a whole ocean, but the Jingwei bird kept working. Some say the Queen Mother of the West gave her a job in her garden, where she still carries twigs and pebbles around.

Below: Symbols of good luck, dragons are commonly found in art and sculpture.

LINK TO TODAY

The woody Lingzhi mushroom is much prized in traditional Chinese medicine. It is eaten in the belief that it can lead to a long and healthy life. Immortality is linked to the mountains where the mushrooms were found.

THE SKIES ABOVE

The Ancient Chinese were keen observers of the sky. They knew a lot about the movements of the Sun, Moon, stars, and planets. Their observations helped them to calculate the length of a month to 29.5 days and a **solar** year to 365.5 days. They noted comets and other heavenly events, and recorded solar and **lunar eclipses** on oracle bones. Myths explained why these events happened: An eclipse was caused by a dragon eating the Sun or Moon.

Many Chinese myths are set in the night sky, the powerful home of the gods. The dragon only makes its appearance in the night sky. One famous myth tells of an animal herder and a spinning goddess—the stars Vega and Altair—whose romance offended the heavens. They were sentenced to meet only once a year, on the seventh day of the seventh month, when a bridge—the Milky Way—forms over the river. This is the time of year when both stars appear high in the night sky.

THE TEN SUNS

The Ancient Chinese paid close attention to the sky. They read signs of heaven's will in the patterns of stars. As far back as the Shang Dynasty, the Chinese people divided time into 10-day weeks. This calculation may relate to the Ten Suns myth, in which the sky must be set right for the people to do their work.

Many years ago, the Emperor of Heaven had 10 sons. It was their duty to take turns shining over heaven. But one day, they all appeared in the sky at the same time. It was so hot that crops shriveled in the fields. People could barely breathe. The king prayed for help and the Emperor of Heaven sent one of his gods, named Yi, to help. At first, Yi wanted only to frighten the suns. He pretended to shoot his red bow, but they did not move. He loaded up a white arrow, pulled back on the bow, and released it. One of the suns exploded into a ball of fire. The blackened remains fell to Earth as a bird. One by one, he shot down the suns until only one arrow remained. The king asked Yi to stop. One sun would be a good thing. Knowing the last arrow was in the king's hands, the sun behaved. Every day, it rises to carry out its duty providing light and heat. Every night, it disappears so people can sleep.

GONG GONG MYTH

When he lost to the Yellow Emperor, power as Earth's ruler Gong Gong was furious. He hit his head against Buzhou Shan, the Incomplete Mountain. This pillar of heaven collapsed. Heaven tilted down and Earth went up. This is believed to be why the stars in China move from east to west and Chinese rivers flow from west to east.

Below: An immortal stands (on the right) among the clouds, looking out over his heavenly palace (shown at the top of the illustration).

DAILY LIFE

In Ancient China, each region had its own king. There were battles as kings fought to overtake neighboring kingdoms and expand their rule. Conquered rulers were allowed to keep their titles but they were required to give service to the winning king.

During this time, there were distinct classes of people. The ruling **nobles** were at the top, followed by soldiers, farmers, workers, and merchants. Even though some merchants were wealthy, they were not regarded as high class. Soldiers in Ancient China were either volunteers, or men who had been forced into the army. Farmers made up most of the population. They worked hard and ended up paying most of what they earned to their landlords.

IMPERIAL OFFICIALS

During Imperial times, Shi Huangdi ruled all of China. His officials— the civil servants—came next in importance. Government officials were those who had passed the exams or who had been born to a noble family. Some officials were rich and of a high class, while others were in lower-level, poor positions. Soldiers rose in social class with their service.

Below: A Xian bronze of an emperor and his chariot.

TOMB OF WEALTH

Lady Dai died of a heart attack in 168 B.C.E. Her tomb reflected the wealth of the Dai family during the Han Dynasty. She was buried with a complete set of silk clothes, Chinese medicine, food, containers of wine and tea, and even musician statues, carved from wood.

NU WA CREATES PEOPLE

Most figures in Chinese myths are male. Males were more highly regarded. Nu Wa is a female goddess. She is the creator of humans in one myth and the mother of humankind in another.

The goddess Nu Wa lived on Earth, but she was the only goddess there and she was lonely. One day, she sat next to a sparkling pond. Looking at her reflection, she thought she would try to make a model of herself from the lakeside mud. It was as perfect a model as only a goddess could make, but even Nu Wa was surprised when she gently set it down on the ground and it began to move. It stood up, sang, and danced, and even called Nu Wa "mother." Nu Wa was so happy, she made another figure, and then another, and another. Each came to life as she set them down. Day after day, Nu Wa had fun creating mud figures and watching them come to life. She then taught these humans to use leaves to cover themselves, to pick fruit to feed themselves, and to gather in the moonlight to celebrate their lives.

Below: A street scene from the Sung capital of Kaifeng around 1150 C.E.

23

THE YELLOW EMPEROR

For thousands of years, one of China's most important political beliefs was that heaven gives its permission to rule only to someone who is worthy of the honor. The Chinese believed that their emperor was the Son of Heaven.

Huangdi was born with the ability to speak. He was chosen to take over from Emperor Shen Nong because he was a clever man and able to control and conquer bad people. As the Yellow Emperor, he reigned not only over people but also over gods and demons. Some say he had four faces, so that he could look in all directions without moving his head. He spent much of his time in heaven, but had a palace on Earth, high in the Kunlun Mountains. In those days, people wore leaves instead of clothes. The Yellow Emperor invented clothes. He taught people to hunt and how to build houses so that they would not need to live in trees. He invented wheeled vehicles to help people travel long distances, and invented medicine to aid the sick. He invented ships to travel the seas and armor to help the warriors. The emperor was a clever and thoughtful leader.

Right: A Han Dynasty **terracotta** figure of a fishmonger from the 3rd century B.C.E. Merchants were treated as ordinary people in Chinese society.

THE FORBIDDEN CITY

Since Shi Huangdi became the First Emperor in 221 B.C.E, China saw the rise and fall of dozens of different emperors. Each one left his own distinct mark on the country. Elaborate tombs, temples, palaces, and other buildings are all associated with imperial rule in China.

One of the most visible reminders of the emperor's supreme rule is the Imperial Palace. It is better known as the Forbidden City, in Beijing, the modern-day capital city of China. Building the palace began in 1406 C.E., soon after the start of the reign of Yongle, the third emperor of the Ming Dynasty. The Forbidden City was the imperial palace and was home to 24 different emperors, whose reigns lasted from 1420 C.E. to 1911 C.E. During this time, entry to the Forbidden City was strictly forbidden to the general public.

The Forbidden City covers 936,000 square yards (782,615 square meters) and contains almost 1,000 different buildings. There are five main gates: the Great Ming Gate, the Gate of Heavenly Peace, the Gate of Origination, the Meridian Gate, and the Gate of Supreme Harmony. Inside the city are three main halls: the Hall of Supreme Harmony, the Hall of Middle Harmony, and the Hall of Preserving Harmony. All of the buildings are arranged evenly on either side of a central line, which is the emperor's imperial route as he proceeds through the city.

STATUS SYMBOLS

In mythical images and carvings, regular dragons are shown with only four toes. Chinese emperors used the five-toed dragon as a symbol of their imperial power. Another symbol of the ruler's power was that only the emperor was allowed to wear the color yellow.

Right: Officials stand in front of the Forbidden City, Beijing, as show on this painting on silk from 1500 C.E.

HOUSES AND HOMES

In Prehistoric China, people roamed the land hunting and gathering their own food. They did not live in permanent shelters but found temporary dwellings in natural shelters, such as caves. Once they began to settle down and grow crops, they began to built simple homes of mud and sticks. They harvested crops of rice and other grains, and mixed these with beans, vegetables, nuts, meat, fish, and shellfish. Evidence that they finished comes from paintings on bowls and the many hooks and net sinkers uncovered by archaeologists. Cooking was done over open fires.

By the time of the Shang Dynasty in Ancient China, soybeans, tea, and mulberries were commonly grown. Village houses were built of wood and stood on hardened earth floors. The walls were covered with a mixture of grasses and mud. Roofs were thatched. Cooking dishes were both functional and decorative.

LINK TO TODAY

Noodles are a common food found throughout the world today. They do not, however, usually keep well for more than a few days after cooking. Archaeologists recently uncovered a bowl of 4,000-year-old noodles alongside the Yellow River in northern China. They were buried beneath 9 feet (2.7 meters) of sediment when a large earthquake and disastrous floods destroyed the ancient village.

Above: City street, such as this one in Beijing, bustled with laborers, merchants, trades, craftworkers, and other people.

In Imperial China, important buildings—such as palaces—were plastered and painted. Bronze household goods included such things as lamps and mirrors. Silk was woven into rich patterns and worn by higher-ranking nobles. Peasants wore clothes made of **hemp**. Layers of material were added for extra warmth during the cold, winter months. Much of the food for farmers—rice, dumplings, fish, and vegetables—was steamed over boiling water on stoves.

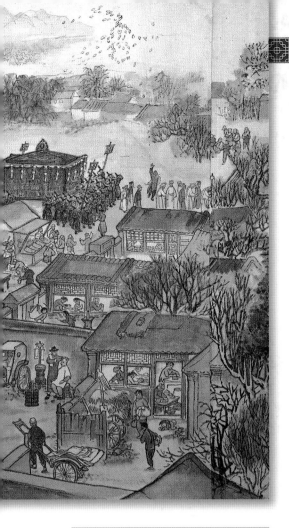

HOW FLINTMAN TAMED FIRE

The Ancient Chinese believed in a wide range of gods and divine rulers. But it was often the actions of people themselves that solved problems, as can be seen in this myth how the flintman tamed fire.

Long ago, people did not know how to use fire. One night, there was huge storm. Lightning lit up the sky and trees caught fire. Hunters went out the next day and found animals beneath fallen trees, their flesh cooked from the heat of the fire. They discovered that cooked meat tasted good and that burning sticks kept wild animals away. They brought back some embers and took turns keeping them burning. If the embers died, they went out into the wilderness to find more.

One day, a young man went and searched for days, but could not find fire. Cold, hungry, and tired, he fell into a deep sleep. In his dreams, an old man told him to go to the Land of the Brightness of Flint and look for a tree. He woke up and set off. Just as darkness fell, he saw a gleam of light ahead. On a branch of a large tree, there was a bird. Every time the bird pecked at the tree, little sparks would fly up. The young man broke off a branch and headed back to his village. He taught people how to use it to make fire whenever they wanted.

FINE FEET

It was the fashion among nobles during the Sung Dynasty for women to bind their feet. To get feet only a few inches long, tight bandages were wound around little girls' feet. The process was painful and walking was also difficult.

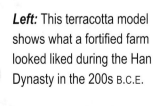

Left: This terracotta model shows what a fortified farm looked liked during the Han Dynasty in the 200s B.C.E.

CALENDARS AND FESTIVALS

During the Shang Dynasty in Ancient China, the day was divided into 12 blocks of two hours each. Weeks contained 10 days. This lunar **calendar** consisted of 12 months—alternating 29 and 30 days—that added up to 364 days in a year. Years went in cycles of 12. Instead of having a number, each year was associated with an animal. The calendar was often reset when a new emperor took power.

Traditionally, Chinese New Year was the most important festival of the year. It began in the middle of the 12th month and ended around the middle of the first. During this time, home and family were

Above: The Chinese New Year Festival includes lighting firecrackers. Some people believe that the noise will scare away evil spirits.

LINK TO TODAY

The Chinese used the lunar calendar until 1911. They still use it today to determine the date of the New Year and other important events. New Year's Day is always on a new moon, but its exact date on the western (solar) calendar varies from late January to early March. The New Year Festival is now often called the Spring Festival.

more important than business. Ritual sacrifices of paper and food were offered to the gods and ancestors, and homes were cleaned to please them. Scrolls with lucky messages were set on household gates. Firecrackers were set off to frighten away evil spirits and other misfortunes.

The festival included lion and dragon dances and parades. Food was also a very important part of the celebration. Long noodles were eaten to **symbolize** long life. On the final day, moon-shaped rice balls were offered as a sign of unity. The last day of the celebrations was the Lantern Festival, when colorful lanterns were hung in houses.

LINK TO TODAY

The Lantern Festival is still practised today. It is believed to date back to the Han Dynasty. One myth tells of how the Jade Emperor was angry at a village because they killed his favorite crane. He planned to destroy the village with fire. A wise man told the villagers to light lanterns and set off firecrackers to fool the emperor, who would think the houses were already on fire. The trick worked, and people continued to light lanterns on that day to give their thanks for being saved.

YI AND CHANG'E

The Mid-Autumn Festival is a celebration of the Moon Goddess. It includes such customs as eating mooncakes, matchmaking, and floating sky lanterns. The Moon rabbit is a traditional icon of Chinese mythology.

Archer Yi was a hero on Earth after shooting the suns from sky, but the Emperor of Heaven was not happy. He wanted his sons brought back to heaven. He told Yi that he was not welcome. Yi's wife, Chang'e, was horrified. She desperately wanted to remain immortal. She heard that the goddess Xi Wang Mu had a potion that could make humans immortal. Chang'e begged Yi to go to Kunlun Mountain. Xi Wang Mu was impressed that a mere human had climbed the mountain and survived. She agreed to give Yi a bit of the potion for him and his wife to take together on a certain date. Only this way could they return to heaven. But Yi's wife was impatient and she took the potion while Yi was gone. Suddenly she was floating, higher and higher into the sky. She knew that she could not go to heaven, for the other gods would think her selfish. She could not go back to Earth because people would think her heartless to leave her husband behind. And so, she flew to the Moon. There she found a rabbit, working on the potion of immortality for Xi Wang Mu.

EDUCATION AND LEARNING

In Ancient China, most of the education was either verbal or hands-on. The main goal of all schooling was to develop deep respect for family and government. Although most people were peasants working in agriculture, and formal education was rare, a fortunate few studied with Confucius. He was a teacher, as well as a great philosopher.

In his private school, male students—girls did not get to go to school —learned the "Six Arts." These arts were charioteering and archery to emphasize physical skills; rituals to enforce a strong moral code; and calligraphy, music, and math to add valuable knowledge. There were many great thinkers in the time of Confucius. His students also studied literature. It was during this time that the first real books were written.

During the Han Dynasty, Emperor Wu Di set up an imperial academy—or high school—in 124 B.C.E. For many years, young men studied the myth-based works of Chinese literature. The Five Classics of the time included the *I Ching* or the "Book of Changes," *The Classic of History*, *The Classic of Poetry*, *The Classic of Rites*, and

The Spring and Autumn Annals. These young men were preparing for the ancient civil service exams. By passing these exams, the men could start jobs with the government or gain promotion in the army.

Below: Male students and their master are shown on this porcelain vase made during the reign of Emperor Kangxi (1661–1722 C.E.).

THE YELLOW EMPEROR'S COMPASS

This epic myth of the battle between the Yellow Emperor and Chi You shows the value of using knowledge and cleverness, instead of magic or strength, to overcome enemies.

The Yellow Emperor ruled people and the spirit world and was constantly challenged for his position. One wicked creature named Chi You wanted to become ruler. Chi You had a man's body but his head was shaped like an ox and made of iron. He was a powerful sorcerer. One day, Chi You gathered some of the monsters of the mountains and demons of the waters and attacked the emperor's palace. Chi You called up a great fog so no one could see. The emperor's forces were forced to withdraw.

But one of the emperor's followers was a clever man named Feng Hou. He made a little chariot with a post in the middle. Mounted on the post was a small figure with one hand extended. As the chariot was turned, the figure moved so that the hand always pointed south. Feng Hou called it a "South-pointing cart." In the next skirmish, Chi You again called up the fog, but the emperor's troops found their way using the chariot and they eventually won the battle.

LINK TO TODAY

The abacus is a "calculating board" developed by the Chinese. It dates back to the period of the Yuan Dynasty of 1280 C.E. to 1368 C.E. The abacus consists of a wooden frame containing rows of movable beads sliding on metal rods. Each bead represents a single unit and can be moved to add, subtract, multiply, and divide. The abacus is sometimes called the first computer because it was used as a model for early computers.

Right: Merchants used the abacus—an ancient calculator—to complete a bill for goods purchased.

Above: This silk painting shows a scene from the play *Romance of the West Chamber* by the Chinese playwright Wang Shifu (1250–1307 C.E.). *Romance of the West Chamber*, a romantic comedy, is his best-known play.

AN ARTISTIC SIDE

Ancient Chinese art included painting, music, sculpture, poetry, and dancing. Music was a part of court life for the emperors and members of the nobility. Calligraphy was a form of handwriting that took many years of practice to master. Using a special brush, characters were drawn clearly, but with artistic expression. When perfected, each individual character —of which there were thousands—was regarded as an art form in itself.

Archaeologists have discovered that, during the time of the Shang Dynasty, people perfected working with bronze. Everything from weapons to armor, pots to stoves, musical instruments to housewares, have been found from this period. They developed molds, which allowed them to make hollow bronze pieces such as pots and urns. The mold could then be reused to make another piece.

Temple walls and palaces were finely painted in Ancient China, although few of these decorations have survived over the years. The Mogao Caves are a Buddhist cave-temple complex dating from the Tang Dynasty. Despite their age, many of the fine religious paintings were found intact on the cave walls.

Art also developed in the process of making pottery. During the Shang Dynasty, potters developed hardwearing, shiny stoneware and glazes. Centuries of creative experimentation saw the evolution of pottery into fine porcelain in the Sui and Tang dynasties. Mythical figures, such as dragons, often decorated the beautifully finished pieces.

CANGJIE CREATES WRITING

Cangjie was an artist with a special talent. The art of writing in China was born because he was able to teach others his system of drawing. Cangjie is honored to this day as the god of writing. He is also the patron of bookmakers, papermakers, and storytellers.

In the time of the Yellow Emperor, the people had much to learn. No one knew how to write, and trying to remember everything was extremely difficult. Fortunately, there lived a man named Cangjie, who was very clever. As a child, he loved to draw pictures. Sometimes he would sit on the river bank and study the markings on the backs of turtles. He would walk in the woods and take note of the patterns on birds' wings. He would wander at night and notice the arrangements of the planets and stars. He took the patterns he saw in nature and drew them out. He found that he could give meanings to the patterns and rearrange them. Finally, he realized that he could communicate with his drawings as well as he could by speaking.

Left: Bamboo is placed into pools of water to form the pulp used to make paper.

PAPER AND PRINTING

Paper was invented in China by Cai Lun in 105 C.E. Cai Lun was an official in the imperial court. He created the first sheet of paper using mulberry and hemp fibers. It took another 700 years before the first engraved wooden blocks were used to print words on paper. Different blocks were carved for each page.

TRADE *AND* WARFARE

Ancient China was geographically isolated for thousands of years. Before China was united under Shi Huangdi, each state had its own system of weights and measures. This made trading between regions within the country very difficult. Standardizing weights and measures not only made sense, but became invaluable when trading was allowed to take place outside of the country.

According to myth, a cocoon one day dropped into the hot drink of the wife of Emperor Shi Huangdi. As the fine threads from the cocoon unraveled, silk was born. China now had a unique treasure that could make the country wealthy. Romans knew China as *Serica* or Land of Silk. Not only did they have silk, but the Chinese also had the riches of salt, tea, lacquerware, bronze, and porcelain. The fine white porcelain was soon to be known as "china."

In exchange for Chinese goods, the Roman Empire traded gold, silver, fine glassware, wine, carpets, and jewels. India traded ivory, textiles, precious stones, and spices, among other goods.

Above: Before standardization, there were many different forms of currency such as these bronze fish-shaped coins from around 300 B.C.E.

TWO-WAY TRADE

Over the centuries, as trade routes formed and grew, more than just valuable cargoes moved west along the Silk Road—the route from Europe to Asia (see page 37). China offered the world unimaginable knowledge and treasures in the form of mathematics, papermaking, the magnetic compass, and gunpowder. In return, they imported a new religion—Buddhism—from India.

THE FIRST SILKWORM

The myth of the First Silkworm teaches the Chinese that a person's promise must be honored at all costs.

A man set off on a journey, leaving his daughter to care for his horse. The girl missed her father. She said that if he could bring her father home, she would marry the horse. The horse jumped up and ran off. The horse found her father, who thought something must be wrong at home. He jumped on the horse and they both returned at a great speed. All was well, and father and daughter were happy to see each other. The horse, however, stayed outside. Over the few days, the father noticed that every time the horse saw his daughter, it jumped and whinnied. He thought this was strange and asked his daughter if she knew what was wrong. She admitted her promise of marriage to the horse. The father was furious. A horse could not marry a human. He shot the horse and left the skin out on the ground. The girl was out playing near the horsehide one day, when it leaped up and covered her and she disappeared. Her father searched and searched, and finally found her hanging in a mulberry tree. She was wrapped in the horsehide and had become a silkworm, busy spinning silk.

THE SILK BUSINESS

Silk fabric was first made in China around 3500 B.C.E. It consisted of woven threads of silk. These were made by caterpillars of the mulberry silk moth building their cocoons. Today, silk is made on a large-scale by several types of insects raised on farms. Nylon is a synthetic, or artificial type of silk.

Right: Silk production was women's work, including weaving the fabric on looms.

During the Qin Dynasty, thousands and thousands of laborers died in the construction of the Great Wall and were buried beneath it. One myth about the wall highlights courage, loyalty, duty, and the bonds of marriage.

One day Meng planted a vine seedling in his yard. The vine grew quickly and spread over the fence to Jiang's yard. Shortly after, Jiang noticed a large gourd. He turned it over and found a baby girl inside. Jiang called her Meng Jiangnu. She became a beautiful, clever, young woman. One day, Meng Jiangnu was in her yard and heard a noise. A young man climbed out of a tree. He had been hiding from forced labor on the Great Wall. The couple fell in love. Several days after their marriage, he was captured and taken away. After her parents died, Meng Jiangnu took the long journey to the Great Wall to find her husband. She discovered that he was dead and buried beneath the stones. She wanted to find his body for a proper burial, but it seemed impossible. She wept uncontrollably, the sound echoing across the mountains. Suddenly there was a large crack and the wall crumbled for miles. Hundreds of skeletons lay exposed. Meng Jiangnu cut her finger and called out to the bones: "If you are husband, my blood is yours." Her blood flowed to one skeleton, and she knew it was her husband.

THE GREAT WALL

The Great Wall stretches for more than 3,100 miles (4,989 kilometers) across northern China. Emperor Shi Huangdi linked together existing fortifications to create one single defensive wall. The wall was built of stone and mud to keep out barbarian tribes from the north.

TRANSPORTING GOODS

The movement of trade goods west from China took many different forms. In some areas, traders could travel in relative comfort in wagons pulled by horses. In harsh desert environments, long caravans of camels were used to carry goods and traders.

As important as trade was, it was more important to have control over who was allowed to enter China. The Great Wall of China is a series of rock and earth fortifications found in northern China. Although most of the existing wall was built during the Ming Dynasty of 1368 C.E. to 1644 C.E., several walls have been built and rebuilt, the most famous being the wall ordered by Shi Huangdi, the First Emperor. Soldiers were stationed at barracks along the wall to defend China's territory.

Shipbuilding technology developed quickly during the Han Dynasty. Sea routes became easier to navigate with the use of the magnetic compass. Coastal settlements quickly became busy ports along the Silk Road. Inland, the Chinese began construction of the 1,050 mile(1,690 kilometer) long Grand Canal during the 400s B.C.E. It took creativity and hard work to build the canal that, today, is still the longest in the world.

Left: Camel drivers worked on the Silk Road during the Tang Dynasty of 618–907 C.E.

THE SILK ROAD

The Silk Road was not actually one route, but a series of interlinking trade routes. The name comes from the Chinese silk trade, which began during the Han Dynasty. Crossing Central Asia, several different branches developed over time. The routes all started from Chang'an in China. The land routes crossed deserts and mountains heading west to the Mediterranean Sea and south toward India. As wells and lakes dried up, the routes would shift over time. The Silk Road also included sea routes from China to Southeast Asia, India, and East Africa.

WARFARE

Warfare is a common theme in Ancient Chinese mythology, being an unpleasant part of life. Different communities and tribes battled for resources, wealth, and power. Early weapons were made of bone, stone, and wood. As bronze, iron, and steel were developed, weapons changed.

In earlier times, between sowing the crops and reaping the harvests Chinese farmers trained with swords and bows and arrows. Over time, the military became more organized. Horse-drawn chariots were driven into battle by trained charioteers, soldiers marched with shields, spears, and javelins, and highly skilled archers increased the range of attack. During the latter part of the Zhou Dynasty, iron armor first appeared. Helmets were made of iron or bronze.

Armies numbered in the hundreds of thousands. There are some estimates that certain states had up to 1 million troops during the Warring States period of the late Zhou Dynasty. Military strategy included battle tactics, as well as spying on the enemy. This was to gather intelligence to win battles without combat.

Shi Huangdi, the First Emperor, was known for his excess. Before his death, he ordered an entire terracotta army built to guard him in the afterlife. This included bowmen, archers, infantrymen, charioteers, and an armored rear guard. They were arranged in military formation. In 1974, farmers digging a well discovered several broken pieces of the almost 7,000 life-like figures.

DEADLY AIM

The crossbow was developed during the 400s B.C.E. The crossbow was accurate, fast, and more deadly than traditional bows. Although firing a crossbow did require a certain amount of training and skill, it was easier for farmers to use when they fought in the army. A crossbow was stretched and cocked with the archer's foot and the arrows smoothly released by a trigger mechanism.

FA MU LAN

Few myths continue to inspire young girls to break traditional roles as much as this story of a woman warrior fighting against all odds. Mu Lan has even become a Disney classic movie. More importantly, this myth teaches the importance of honor and obedience.

The emperor needed more soldiers. Every family was required to send someone to serve in the imperial army. It was a matter of honor and Mr. Fa was worried. He was too old and frail. His son was far too young. His daughter, Mu Lan, convinced the family that she should go. She was trained in martial arts and was a strong fighter. The family, knowing there was no other choice, agreed. Dressing like a soldier, Mu Lan entered the army and fought with honor, disguised as a man for many years. As a reward for her service she asked for nothing more than to be allowed to return home. When she did return, she put on women's clothes and returned to the life expected of a lady, never forgetting the freedoms she was able to experience as a man.

Left: Shi Huangdi's terracotta army contains almost 7,000 life-sized figures that were built to guard the emperor in his afterlife.
Right: This Mongol warrior from 1200s C.E. is armed with a bow, lance, and saber.

LINK TO TODAY

Flying a kite is a fun pastime today, but kites began as weapons of war. Kites originated with the Chinese military during the Han Dynasty. Kites were flown over enemy lines to measure distances for attack. They were also used to signal messages.

CHINESE LEGACY

Ancient Chinese myths have become woven into the fabric of modern society. Many ceremonies and festivals originate from these ancient stories.

The Dragon Boat Festival is a holiday held on the fifth day of the fifth month of the Chinese year. According to myth, the festival honors the death of the poet Qu Yuan during the Zhou Dynasty. When Qin's army took control of China, Qu Yuan drowned himself. Admirers dropped rice cakes into the river to feed the poet in his afterlife. When fish nibbled on the cakes, they paddled out to scare the fish away. The Double Fifth or Dragon Boat Festival is now an annual celebration and dragon-boat races are held around the world.

Another popular festival is the Night of Sevens Festival. This commemorates the forbidden love of the mythical stars Vega and Altair (see page 20). It is often known today as Chinese Valentine's Day.

Many other Chinese myths show great respect for such things as loyalty to family, hard work, self-sacrifice, wisdom, and power. These traits are as admired today as they were in ancient times.

ANCESTOR WORSHIP

Ancient Chinese worshiped their ancestors. Today's Lantern Festival honors deceased relatives. The festival centers on getting the family back together, and on peace and forgiveness. Small rice balls filled with nuts and fruit are eaten. The round shape of this treat symbolizes wholeness and unity within the family, which is as important now as it was in the early days of Confucianism.

Below: Traditional paper lanterns are lit during festivals to guide home the spirits of the dead.

HOW YU TAMED THE FLOOD

Yu the Great was the first emperor of the mythical Xia Dynasty. According to a myth, he stopped the rising waters of a river, saved the people, and fulfilled his father's wishes. Honoring one's parents is important in Chinese culture even today.

A long time ago, the Celestial Emperor became displeased with the people. He sent a great flood to wipe them out. Gun was a grandson of the Celestial Emperor. He felt sorry for the people, so he stole one of the emperor's treasures: mud and dirt that reproduced itself. Heading to Earth, he cast the dirt about and the flood was stopped. The emperor was furious. He ordered the gods of fire to kill Gun and bring back the dirt. The flood started again. Gun's body would not disappear because his job was not finished. A baby dragon started to grow inside his stomach. Hearing of this strange pregnancy, the Celestial Emperor sent a servant to cut open Gun's belly. Out flew Yu. Yu told the emperor that he must finish his father's work. The emperor was so impressed, that he lent Yu the magical dirt. Reaching Earth, Yu flung the dirt all around and the flood was stopped.

Left: The Golden Sand River racing through Tiger Leaping Gorge shows the mass of sediment in the flood waters.

LINK TO TODAY

Flooding is a common theme in Chinese mythology. It is also a common event in modern-day China. The Yellow River begins in the Kunlun Mountains and flows more than 3,100 miles (4,989 km). Muddy waters deposit **sediment** near the end of the river's journey to the sea, raising the level of the riverbed. Chinese laborers build dikes and dredge canals to keep the river on course.

THE STUDY CONTINUES

Scholars continue to study Ancient Chinese myths in hope of gaining further understanding of their meaning. Archaeologists use mythology to help them understand the artifacts they uncover. Artists explore the connections between past and present.

Ai Weiwei is a famous Chinese artist who creates artworks by taking ancient artifacts and adding modern touches. He painted a Han Dynasty urn with the Coca-Cola® logo and broke apart pieces of Imperial Chinese furniture and rearranged them in odd shapes. Ai Weiwei became an international success. However, his methods of promoting art and comments about government control resulted in a two-month prison sentence. During his time in prison, his latest bronze sculptures were shown in London and New York. They are based on animal heads from the signs of the Chinese zodiac. Artistic freedom—in art or writing or speech—is something Ai Weiwei is passionate about.

LINK TO TODAY

Feng shui is the ancient art of placing objects and balancing color in order to create a sense of balance and harmony in everyday life. The central idea behind feng shui is that energy flows from every living and non-living object. This is nothing new. The Ancient Chinese also believed that matter and energy were the same things.

Left: This Chinese Imperial arch was built thousands of miles from China in the Canadian capital of Ottawa. It has features similar to the Imperial Palace at the Forbidden City. It shows how Chinese design has spread around the modern world.

Left: People dressed as giant puppets roam the streets during the Chinese Ghost Festival.

FIREWORKS

Fireworks were invented by the Ancient Chinese. Chemicals such as potassium nitrate and sulfur were mixed with finely ground charcoal to make a black, flaky powder that burned with a loud bang when it was ignited. The Chinese called it *huo yao* or "fire chemical." Today we call it gunpowder, and it is used to create the spectacular lights and noise of fireworks. Different mixes of chemicals produce the various colors, from red, blue, and green, to brilliant white.

Left: Fireworks came from China but are now used around the world.

左: 张艺谋武侠巨制

Left: The poster for a Chinese film *House of Flying Daggers*, based on an Ancient Chinese myth.

Right: Mahjong is a Chinese game of skill that is played around the world.

INFLUENCING THE WORLD

Every time you sip tea from a china cup, watch movies made by Chinese filmmakers such as *Raise the Red Lantern* and *Yellow Earth*, take a lesson in Tai Chi, or paddle in a dragon-boat race, you can see what a large impact Chinese culture has had on our world today.

Many people play the Chinese game of Mahjong. Similar to dominoes, the tiles are engraved with Chinese symbols and characters. The name comes from the word *maque,* or sparrow. The sparrow or a mythical "bird of one hundred intelligences" is found on one of the tiles.

Reading your horoscope—a forecast of your future—is a popular pastime. According to Chinese myths, Buddha asked all the animals to join him on Chinese New Year. Twelve came. Buddha named a year after each one. According to the Chinese zodiac, if you were born in the year of the dragon, you have that animal's characteristics (the others being a monkey, pig, tiger, ox, rat, rooster, dog, snake, horse, sheep, or rabbit).

Ancient Chinese mythology set the groundwork for many things in our world today that we take for granted. Think about it the next time you give your father a silk tie, or help hang Chinese lanterns in the garden, or learn about Chinese medicine.

In the words of Confucius: "Study the past if you would define the future."

TIME CHART

1,700,000 years ago–2205 B.C.E. **PREHISTORIC CHINA**

2953–2205 B.C.E. The Mythical Rulers and the Five Emperors

2698–2599 B.C.E. Reign of Huangdi, the Yellow Emperor

2357–2205 B.C.E. Reigns of Emperors Yao and Shun

2206–221 B.C.E. **ANCIENT CHINA**

2205–1766 B.C.E. Xia Dynasty

1766–1121 B.C.E. Shang Dynasty

1121–221 B.C.E. Zhou Dynasty

550 B.C.E. Confucius born

221 B.C.E.**–1911** C.E. **IMPERIAL CHINA**

221–206 B.C.E. Qin Dynasty

221–210 B.C.E. Reign of First Emperor Shi Huangdi

214–206 B.C.E. Great Wall first built

206 B.C.E.**–220** C.E. Han Dynasty

106 C.E. Invention of paper

220–280 Three Kingdoms

265–420 Jin Dynasty

420–479 Song Dynasty

479–589 The Six Dynasties

589–618 Sui Dynasty

618–907 Tang Dynasty

907–960 The Five Dynasties and Ten Kingdoms

960–1280 Song Dynasty

1280–1368 Yuan (Mongol) Dynasty

1368–1644 Ming Dynasty

1406–1420 Forbidden City built

1644–1911 Qing (Manchu) Dynasty

1911– present REPUBLICAN CHINA

1911 Republic of China founded

1949 Chinese Communists take power

GLOSSARY

ancestor A family member who lived a long time ago

Ancient China Period of Chinese history from 2205 B.C.E. to 221 B.C.E., when the country was ruled by kings

artifact An ancient object made by humans

calendar A chart showing the year divided into months, weeks, and days

civil servants People who work for the government and run the country

crane Large wading bird with long neck and legs

culture The arts, customs, and ideas of a particular country

eclipse The obscuring or hiding of a star, moon, or planet by another

empire A part of the world ruled over by an emperor and contains many previously independent countries

festival A day or period of time set aside for celebration

god or goddess A male or female heavenly being who is worshiped

hemp A plant with tough fibers that are used to make rope and canvas

immortality Life that goes on forever

Imperial China Period of Chinese history between 221 B.C.E. and 1911 C.E., when the country was ruled by emperors

kingdom Country ruled over by a king

legacy Something handed down to a successor

lunar Relating to the Moon

mortality Life that ends in death

myth An old story that explains everyday events and things, often including supernatural beings

mythical Relating to a myth

mythology The myths of a country or people

noble A high-ranking, titled person

Prehistoric China Period of Chinese history from 1.7 millions years ago until 2205 B.C.E.

ritual A religious or other ceremony in which certain actions are performed in a strict order

sacrifice Killing of a person or animal as an offering to a god

sediment Solid matter that is carried along by a river and eventually settles on the river bed

solar Relating to the Sun

symbolize To represent or stand for something

temple A place of worship

terracotta A brownish-red earthenware made of clay and used to make pottery and statues

trade The business of buying and selling goods

traditions Customs that are passed on from one generation to another

warfare The act of conducting war with another people or nation

LEARNING MORE

BOOKS

Challen, Paul. *Hail! Ancient Chinese* (Hail! History). St. Catharines, ON: Crabtree Publishing, 2011.

Challen, Paul. *Life in Ancient China* (Peoples of the Ancient World). St. Catharines, ON: Crabtree Publishing, 2005.

Conover, Sarah, et al. *Harmony: A Treasury of Chinese Wisdom for Children and Parents.* Spokane: Eastern Washington University Press, 2008.

Cotterell, Arthur. *Ancient China.* (Eyewitness Books.) New York: DK Publishing, Inc., 2005.

Kleeman, Terry, and Tracy Barrett. *The Ancient Chinese World.* New York: Oxford University Press, 2005.

Van Pelt, Todd, and Rupert Matthews. *Ancient Chinese Civilization.* New York: Rosen Central, 2009.

Shuter, Jane. *Ancient China.* Chicago: Heinemann Library, 2006.

Xuegang Sun, and Cai Guoyun. *Chinese Myths.* New York: Viking Press, 2008.

WEBSITES

History for Kids—Ancient China
www.historyforkids.org/learn/china/

Ancient China for Kids
http://china.mrdonn.org/

The Ancient Web: The Ancient Chinese Civilization
http://ancientweb.org/explore/country/China

History of China (video links)
www.neok12.com/History-of-China.htm

Condensed China: Chinese History for Beginners
http://condensedchina.com/

British Museum: Ancient China
www.ancientchina.co.uk/menu.html

[Website addresses correct at time of writing—they can change.]

INDEX